HAVE FAITH

JOHN S. RHODES

COPYRIGHT

© Copyright 2023 John S. Rhodes. All Rights Reserved.

This book may not be reproduced or transmitted in any form without the written permission of the publisher. Although the author and publisher have prepared this book with the greatest of care, and have made every effort to ensure its accuracy, we assume no responsibility or liability for errors, inaccuracies, or omissions. There will certainly be mistakes in grammar, typography, or content. Apologies in advance.

Table of Contents

PART I

What Is Faith?
Why Does Faith Matter?
Who Has Faith?
Where Does Faith Come From?

PART 2

Your Faith
Know The Truth
Holding Truth
Your Deep Belief
Ready to Receive
Faith Always And Everywhere

PART I

What Is Faith?

Faith is not a thing. It's not an object.

This should come as a great relief because most people tend to think they need to have faith. Most people feel strongly that they need to grab on. But, it's fleeting. It pours through your fingers like grains of sand. Faith cannot be held in the hands.

I know that I was challenged by this for many years. I thought I had failed because I could not have faith. I could not own it. I didn't feel strong enough to flex my muscles to grab and hold faith.

But, my friend, please feel the relief. Let it wash over you. Faith is impossible to hold on to because it isn't an object. It's not a thing.

The revelation is simple. Faith is a process.

As you will soon discover, there is a simple and very specific process for understanding faith. This process will also give you more faith, in all areas of your life. It's really quite simple.

Now, for a quick moment, consider how many problems we face in philosophy, science, religion and many of the "deep" things we care about. For example, many people believe we must discuss the mind or the body, as if they are separate. Still others believe we must discuss the soul or the brain. Again, as if they are separate. What you will discover later on is that the process of faith gives us a way to solve these types of challenges.

Ultimately, because faith is a process, and a way of being, you can easily get results. You can easily see and feel faith. It can be an object or a thing, in a sense. While this seems to contradict what I explained a moment ago, consider that unknown destinations are like clouds. They come and go. But, if you take a carefully planned trip, when you get to the location, you have arrived at a very specific, very real place.

Therefore, faith must begin as a process but it becomes more and more real over time. The more you understand and use faith as a process, the more it becomes solid, almost as if you can touch it. In fact, I believe that this alone explains many religious experiences. I also believe this explains the visceral nature of many scientific discoveries and profound philosophies.

Honestly, I find even talking this way about faith electrifies me. I think faith is fascinating and I hope you are ready for what comes next on our path together. And, by the way, if you're experiencing deja vu right now, that's common because you've already started the faith process.

Why Does Faith Matter?

Here's the funny thing about faith. If you don't have faith in something, then your life has far less meaning. You feel more pain. Your endurance is lower. You don't see colors as brightly. All of this is to say, without some faith, you are drifting on the ocean. Life lacks meaning.

Let me tell you a quick story. I once had this dream that I was in outer space. Everything was fine at first. Then, the ship was suddenly gone, and I was drifting along in my space suit. Now I was floating. The stars were incredible. Then, I was struck by sheer terror because there was nothing to latch onto, no one to reach, and nothing I could do. I learned a deep, valuable lesson.

Without faith, you are everything and nothing, all at once.

When there is zero faith, the foundations of reality start to crack a bit. Everything is suddenly on your shoulders. There's no higher power. No reference points. And worse, there's no real history, and no way back to any grounding. The foundation is gone. Chaos and darkness reign supreme, forever and ever.

Now, I have to stop here for a moment. I'm not calling out any religion, religious power or even a deity. I respect you, exactly as you are, and exactly where you stand. My essential point here is that when there is no process of faith, there is no real faith. And without faith, principles are minimized, even lost completely.

Here's an example. If you don't believe in stop signs, and other people don't believe in stop signs, or any of the laws behind stop signs, or any type of law enforcement regarding stop signs, doesn't this overall lack of belief allow for chaos to reign? For a better, more positive life, we need to believe in stop signs. What they are and what they do. After all, something must bind the rules and laws together in our world. This is how belief binds the nonphysical to the physical. And, to continue with our example, we also need to believe in law enforcement and even the process of creating the laws that make stop signs work. In short, belief is the antidote to chaos.

So, the very structure of your reality depends on believing things. But, more importantly, getting that structure, depends on the process or the path.

Here's another analogy for fun. I can give you a blueprint, materials, and tools. I can give you workers. I can yell and scream. I can pay people. But, if there isn't true action, the house cannot and will not be built. And make no mistake, the house cannot be built unless you have everything I've mentioned, including the time and effort applied. To be even more clear, the blueprint isn't the process, it's real people, using materials and tools, following the blueprint.

Now, what if I told you that these blueprints, materials and tools exist all around you, right now. And, what if I also told you that taking action is precisely how faith is manifested.

Through the process of faith, many problems in your life are removed. In fact, when done right, as I will continue to explain, this applied faith will heal nearly any person. That's simply because the actions of faith automatically generate love. And, as we have all experienced, love is the eternal power that minimizes pain and erases hate.

Love expressed is faith. Trust me, we'll come back to this later on, if you stick with me. What you must understand now is that while this love is everywhere, it does also have direction. That is because of how love is expressed, which brings us to the next critical topic.

Who Has Faith?

Everyone has faith. The answer is both simple and surprising. So, I want to make sure several things are very clear.

I first need to stress again that faith does not need to be religious. It can be scientific, mathematical or philosophical. It can be deep and cosmic, and it can be plain and pedestrian. It's critical to avoid strongly connecting faith with any one specific thing. In fact, this is what blinds the most devout, while making faith invisible to those outside of any dogma or practice.

I will count on you to have an open mind for now. The key here is that you must understand the process of faith to have faith. Once the doors and windows are properly opened, you can apply your new awareness to nearly everything in your life.

If you feel you have strong faith right now then consider backing away from what you hold so dear. Do not abandon what faith you have, just elevate yourself above what you see as your faith right now. In this case, it's fine to think of faith as a thing, so you can work around it, work through it, and work with faith.

Remember, faith is a process. It becomes more and more of a thing or an object as action is taken in the right way.

Returning to the core, everyone that I know has faith in something. Often, on the surface, you will have faith in your family and friends. You believe in them. You trust they will be there for you.

As a hint of what's to come, when someone close to you takes action in line with your expectations, your faith gets a boost. Your feelings are amplified. You know exactly the good feelings I'm explaining here. When someone "comes through" for you there is joy, and love.

I now need to deflate the balloon just a bit. I realize expectations are high and you might deeply resonate with what I'm saying here. That's very common and you're in good company. But, here's the truth about faith. We feel there is never enough. I have to give you an example now.

Remember as a kid you would look off in the distance and see the horizon? Usually, you would be on flat land, maybe walking, riding a bike or enjoying your time on a skateboard or scooter. You would move toward the horizon, but you would never make it. Ever! Most kids quickly internalize this. They realize they can move toward the horizon as a "thing" but they never get there. It's not possible.

Now consider every move you make toward the horizon. I bet you feel like it's still real, but deep in your mind, you know it's not a true destination. Yet, you also know down to your bones that the journey you're taking toward the horizon is very real. You have faith that there is a horizon, but you also know you will never get there. It's real, but wait, it's not. This is profound.

The key to everything about faith is the framework. It's the concepts. It's the experience you have, and how

you even build reality. You believe in
your experience. You believe in
things that are simultaneously real,
but can never be reached.

Some people at this point start to feel
odd sensations. It's also very
common to be visualizing your
childhood in a very emotional way.
That's because earlier I spoke of your
early life experience and created a
new context for you.

In other words, you have been forced
to believe in two things at once that
are nearly opposite: the horizon as a
thing that's real and the horizon as
something that you will never reach,
no matter how much time and effort
you apply. Then, you took these two

concepts, and put yourself in that world we created, and this world we are in together, outside your mind.

This realization is also part of the process of faith. It's these kinds of steps we all must take, in all parts of our lives, to fully grasp the truth of both infinity and zero. While that's another topic, it's worth noting here that infinity and zero are the same. Consider that if something is infinite it never ends and never stops. That means it is also a starting point from nothing. It's zero. There's more to the story, but it's a good way to bend your thinking.

Getting back on track, here is another truth to ponder. Because faith is a process, and a never-ending journey, there can be some frustration. After all, if you cannot firmly grasp faith, but only make progress, there's a longing for more. In large part, this is the genesis of desire. You want more, and that's natural. The cup can fill your entire life, but never quite get full. You cannot have a truly "full cup" of faith, although you could get closer and closer over time.

Here's a final piece to consider. I mentioned that faith is directional. It's actually like a vector in that it has both a direction and a magnitude. In math, that magnitude is length. Think of it here in relation to how far your mind, heart, body and soul can reach. Bigger thoughts usually have greater reach. Bigger thoughts last longer too. You feel this and know this.

That's why the direction of faith matters. You can go almost infinitely outward with the process. What most forget is that you can also go almost infinitely inward. Some people lose their way. They get lost in the clouds or they get sucked into the depths. This is not a bad thing whatsoever, as long as the destination of these nearly infinite journeys comes back to center. I'll let you own that, in the best way possible. I will continue forward with that now firmly in place.

Where Does Faith Come From?

I'm happy to report that you are already fully aware of where to find faith. You have seen for yourself that faith is a process and the destination can never be reached. But, every step forward increases the knowledge and awareness of faith itself, if it could somehow be held.

There is a saying by Idowu Koyenkan that says, if you quit on the process, you are quitting on the result. As this relates to faith, if you don't stay on your journey, then you are quitting on faith itself. Even if you cannot reach faith, like you would for a

Disney vacation, you shouldn't give up on the dream. You should not let the desire burn out.

The process of faith cannot be static. It's like a motorcycle full of gas just sitting there. Even with a rider and a map, the journey needs to happen for the manifestation.

It's true that dreams can provide inspiration. Meditation and prayers are likewise useful, since action is being taken. But, returning to the vector idea, without real movement then there is far less faith.

Let's use an analogy. If you dream of basketball, that's fuel. That's inspiration. If you think deeply about playing basketball, that's powerful too, much like meditation and prayer might work for some. But, these processes all face inward. It's good, but it's merely half of reality.

To increase faith, outward action is required. So, while it's true a basketball player can get better without playing, full improvement can only happen by actually playing basketball. The player must play. The actor must act. The singer must sing. The faithful must enact faith.

Notice that I have not put any strong emphasis on how to actually have faith. I think you'll agree that I've taken the focus off having faith in favor of focusing on the process of faith. That's because you now know that true faith comes from doing faith.

Indeed, perhaps the best way to think about it is this. You want to "be" faith. I'm not talking about being faithful, although that's obviously important. I'm talking about both the inward process of faith and the outward process of faith.

Think on faith, act on faith. Be the embodiment of faith. You do this all at once. It's then, and only then, that you can "be" faith itself. That's when you finally have faith in your heart.

I am not trying to be melodramatic about this. For an individual, exactly like you, I'm really saying that the inward process of faith is the mind. The outward process of faith is the body. Doing both in harmony creates bliss, happiness and love, in most cases. Energy is rightly focused. You know this already. It's why the process of your faith is so personal and emotional.

When done right, the process of inward plus outward expression of faith builds an incredible fortress, brick by brick. That castle will never be complete. And, ironically, despite the incredible strength and power, the doors and windows will be open to all. You build a free and open fortress. How truly incredible!

The perplexity here is that this is so obvious when you see, hear it, and visualize it.

What's truly incredible is that this is also so easy now to explain to others. You can share your realization of the process of faith with others in just a few sentences. This expression, in turn, further reveals even higher levels of faith. It's always onward and upward. This is love.

If you're dizzy at these heights, trust me, I understand. Those around me often get so much energy from these discussions that they cannot stop asking questions. They can't stop smiling and enjoying the breakthrough.

In a few cases, those around me are stunned silent. That's also very rational and deeply moving, because you can see the gears in the mind turning. The inward processes of faith are suddenly turned on. This is a power surge like no other.

I promised this would be short. And, I was planning on stopping at this point since the essential points have been covered. Everything here is simple, yet you can go through this again and again. Each time, something new will appear before your eyes. That's the process of the process! Do you see? Do you understand?

I won't stop quite yet. I realized something absolutely critical, and that's that you probably need what everyone needs. Right now, more than anything, and despite all that's been revealed, you need the starting point, and you need a way to build your own proven faith process.

While faith itself is a well known concept, the process of faith, of "being" faith, is absolutely new to millions of people. Therefore, in what follows in Part 2, I promise to show you exactly where to start, and exactly how to build your own personalized faith in the spirit that best matches what's on your mind and in your heart.

PART 2

Your Faith

There's a great book by Simon Sinek called Find Your Why. Simply put, the central idea is that you need to know your purpose before you do anything else. Your why is your higher purpose that inspires you, and acts as the source of everything you do.

I largely agree with this. The challenge is that many people simply do not know their why. They don't feel that they know their purpose.

While there are plenty of tools and exercises to help you find your why, they still miss a larger point.

You want to know your why but you actually want to know why you have that why. You want to know why you are the way you are. You want to know where you are from? There is one why after another, always stacking up.

So, I love the power of knowing your why. But, it's like a fractal, or those dolls you open up only to reveal another smaller doll inside.

What if instead you try treating your why like we now treat faith. In other words, what if your reason why is the journey itself. That's right, you've probably just guessed it.

Your reason why is life itself.

I'd like you to consider that life is the answer not the question. It's not about why are you here. It's not about where you are from. Instead, it's flipped. You are here, and you create the best why possible.

This is a radical idea. It's also critical to remember that all life is in motion. You are living right now. You are experiencing these words. What you are doing and thinking, right this very second, is all part of your reason why. You're building it. You're experiencing it.

Here's the great cherry on top. Everyone around you is doing the exact same thing as you. They are in the process of life. Therefore, just like you, they are smack dab in the middle of faith, because faith is a process. They are looking inside, they are looking outside. They are acting. They are doing. They are being faith in motion, just like you.

Are you seeing more clearly now? This is very much the brotherhood. This is sisters united. This is family ties. This is leadership, courage and hope. Of course, when done wrong, it's frustration, stress and worry. And, sometimes worse.

Our current state, our current affairs, are faith in motion. Our why is the starting point of our faith. We are connecting with faith nonstop, like an electric fan plugged into the wall. We are both juiced, and we are juicing. We are the energy.

Don't be afraid but you are the why.

Start with yourself. Start with your why.

Begin the process of faith. It's up to you.

Know The Truth

This is beautiful.

When you understand that "being" in the process of faith is the way to truth, you get much closer to truth itself. You're the living instance of faith, for yourself, and for others.

While you cannot be everything to everyone, you can be an instance of truth. The longer you're on your path, and the more you live on the path, the more you become the path itself.

Recall that the journey is the key here. Every step forward gives you something that cannot be replaced. I'm talking about your experience. The implications are enormous.

While you cannot ever reach the horizon you can understand what it is. You know the meaning, even without touching it. Ever. In stark contrast, at any time, you can look around and see life right near you. You can even see yourself. You are right there.

So, when you look around, or look back, you not only understand life in this instant, but also the exact path you've taken. It's all as real as your life, no tricks.

What makes all this better is that you go from a potentially fuzzy idea of your "why" to a crystal clear understanding of truth. And, it's your truth, that no one can ever take from you.

Think about it. You know the truth. It's so concrete. So wonderful. In just one simple step, you go from your why right into your life, and you have immediate, real truth. This is exactly why action brings your faith alive. And yes, of course, I'm talking about your literal and real faith.

This faith, like your truth, and your life as it is right now, cannot be taken from you. This is exactly how your faith is bedrock. I strongly urge you to consider how much love this creates.

When you aren't shackled to false beliefs, you logically have more freedom. And, when you reflect on your life, and your truth, what other people are doing and saying doesn't have to change your faith whatsoever. Now, if you want your faith to change, and improve, then you accept this into your life. But, if there are lies and deception, then your faith will prevail.

Why? You must understand exactly why this is true. It's because many other people think they are holding faith. They think they own faith, like they would hold a bowling ball or pair of shoes. But you know, deeply and truly, that since faith is a process, it cannot be held as a thing.

If this doesn't give you the armor you want and need, I honestly don't know how to break through. Because you now have a simple way to be kind and generous to people even when their faith doesn't line up with what you believe, and how you act.

Others are trying to use faith like a blunt object. You are "being" faith, you are living life and embracing faith as a process. And, that process is personal, although family and friends matter in your life.

Now wait until you see what comes next. I've already hinted a bit and perhaps you've made a guess, but it's still much bigger than what you could have possibly imagined.

Holding Truth

Many people think of holding as a physical action or a mental action. For example, you might hold a glass of water in your hand. Or, you might hold a phone number in your mind. It's very natural to think of holding as something that you do. But now, here's the huge shift.

Holding truth is the act of being truthful. Likewise, having faith is the action of being faithful. Like you have already seen many times now, if you strongly desire faith, then you need to see the path, walk the path, and even be the path itself.

You "take" the journey but you are the journey at the exact same time. You are the life. You are therefore holding life, including the truth, including faith.

The special twist here is that the harder you try to hold faith, as typically explained, the harder it becomes over time. The effort to hold faith, in the traditional sense, is very difficult. Some would even say faith becomes a burden.

Perhaps you've heard this. Perhaps you've felt this. In the old way of thinking, it's very much much like Sisyphus, the figure from Greek mythology who is forced to forever roll a boulder up a hill, but never reaching the top.

The boulder of faith, because it's too often treated as a thing, gets heavy. It's no wonder so many people suffer a crisis of faith. The weight is tremendous when this is how it's understood.

But, now you have no such burden. The pressure and stress are gone. That's because you clearly understand that faith is a process. It's part of life. You might even think of faith as life itself, and you are both at the center of it all, but also almost nothing. You are light as a feather, floating in the wind. Life around you will carry you along, like a breeze.

What you must hold isn't a thing. You must hold the way. You must hold the process. You must continue on your path. You must build the path, but let it fall behind you, as history, as you move forward. Of course, to your delight, you can look back at any point. You can even time travel with faith this way, by returning to special points in the past. What a relief. What a joy.

You now see that faith is built and it's held easily. Not because of an iron grip or like some mental gimmick for memorization. Instead, holding both truth and faith is done with every little action forward in your life. Eyes open, mind aware.

it gets better because this also means that since you're living your life, acting in faith, it's very physical and real. It's certainly not just mind, or mental. It's also physical. You literally can feel faith in your body. Literally feel faith in your heart.

Holding faith this way is so profound that you might shudder with joy and excitement. As you think about it, your faith increases, because you're mentally moving forward.

But wait, consider that when you explain this others, your action physically creates faith in the real world. I'm talking about lips, tongue, lungs but also sound waves, ears, and more. Your faith flows mentally and physically to others.

I understand that by this point many of your core beliefs about faith have been shattered. Do not fear, do not back down. This is merely what happens as you gain enlightenment. It's also natural to challenge these changes. It's a safety mechanism to protect yourself. So, do not fret, but instead put aside the time to ponder, and embrace. This isn't a race.

You are now ready for the next transformation. Prepare yourself.

Your Deep Belief

I first must summarize a few points, very quickly. First, life itself is your reason why. You are in a constant state of faith through actions and experience. Faith is a journey. Second, having faith is a way of life. Faith isn't possessed, it's a personal process. Third, holding faith is done by living your life. It's not mental or physical, it's physical and mental. Explaining this to others creates even more faith, because actions of faith build more faith in yourself, in others, and the world.

With this in your mind, there is a special way to easily enjoy faith. That is, you can certainly experience faith as I've described, but you can almost always enjoy your faith, even when times are tough, or you feel like you are in a deep, dark cave. This will give you hope in troubled times.

I'm talking about a simple practice. But, before I reveal this, it's critical that you take the previous points above to heart, so to speak. You must understand and agree that faith is a process, and not a thing, otherwise you fall into various traps, such as greed, envy and fear.

Let go of your notion that faith is a thing but instead understand why it must be a process if you wish to succeed with faith in your life. Indeed, again, faith is your life, and

life if your faith. Keeping it simple, positive action is positive faith.
That's the foundation.

You are ready for the simple practice. To easily enjoy faith you need to believe you already have faith. That's it. Just because this is simple, don't think it's easy. Staying calm is a simple idea, except when someone is yelling at you. Putting on a smile is a simple act, except when someone is angry around you. Having self-discipline is a simple practice, except when you see and smell the chocolate chip cookies on the table while you are on a diet. Do you see?

So, the simplicity is powerful. Believe you have faith. Feel your faith. Know your faith. Embrace life with faith in your mind and on your lips. Live a life of faith. If you truly know you are acting on faith, and that you're acting through faith, then you will have more faith.

Actions of faith create more actions of faith. Faith creates faith. Just remember, that the process of faith is not the same as some thing or some object of faith. Faith is living, faith is being.

Again, you must believe. Belief is an action. It's a transfer of energy. In some ways, it can be energy itself. It never goes away completely, or down to zero. As long as there's action and movement there is the potential for growing faith.

This explains why faith is infinite. Life is infinite. Parts of you are infinite. Indeed, perhaps you are entirely infinite, as an infinite part of the whole, or maybe a whole part of what is infinite. Do not worry if that is too deep. It's just a reminder that faith is abundant. It's infinitely abundant. Peace, my friend!

At the risk of "going off the rails" I will also add that a deep belief in faith also allows you to bend reality. I do not wish to argue with you or anyone about this. Instead, I want you to just consider that if you hold the process of faith in your mind and body, and you take action, it's only logical that your acts of faith bend reality. I might tone it down with some people and say that acts of faith shape reality. That's fine too.

The very deep point here is worth your time. You have the ability to develop an incredible abundance of faith. So much faith, in fact, that you are the source of faith for others. Of course, you cannot replace their faith. You cannot "be" all their faith. That's arrogance. But, it's only sensible that faith flows down into you, out of you, and into the worth. Faith is shared.

Think of how sports fans share their enthusiasm and energy. Faith is profoundly similar. Fans don't just think about sports, or their teams, or favorite players. Fans also cheer and applaud. Fans smile at each other. Fans enjoy the entirety of the events. It's infectious. Now, slightly adjust your thinking and it becomes obvious that faith, as an action, or set of actions, creates more faith.

It all starts with a firm belief in faith. You must not only picture those action of faith you have taken, and will take, but you must also know that your thoughts and actions of faith shape faith all around.

If you are skeptical, if you don't believe in faith as an action, absolutely nothing will allow you to have faith. Consider this too. Other people living in faith might shower you with energy. They might speak. They might be joyous and loving. But, even if you experience that faith, you may not be able to continue on that path. Ultimately, you are the key in your own faith. That's because you must live that faith, because it is action. It's your life. It's energy transformation; eternal flow. Sounds "big" but it's remarkably simple.

As a quick caution before moving on, I strongly encourage you to discuss faith as a process. But, unless those around you believe in faith as a process, and faith as living life, then you are at risk of spreading negativity. You are forcing something on someone else who isn't ready, or does not wish to be ready. That is not your burden. And, very importantly, what you see as a "lack of faith" is your view and your choice. You might be wrong. There could be many, many reasons another person isn't ready, or able to embrace faith as a journey.

I ask you to be thankful for challenges. I encourage you to embrace the frustration. You see, the obstacle is the way. Not to change others. Instead, to change yourself. Living your faith, living your life full of faith demands simplicity. If it takes complexity or tremendous effort, then that's life itself giving you strong clues.

Water finds its low point. The principles and process should lead you to the path of least resistance, not greater resistance. We move from high to low. We keep getting better, faster and stronger in faith over time. It should get easier, not harder. Find better analogies. Use better approaches. Be a better example. All of this is a win for you because your faith improves.

Ready to Receive

I will continue to assume that you are feeling more faith as you enjoy one breakthrough after another. I will also assume that you are on the watch so that you're not trying to hold onto faith. Instead, you're living life, living your faith, and being faithful as a process.

With that context, if you visualize faith in your mind, and feel it in your body, there is clarity. There is purpose. You are feeling better, you are sharing. It's even bigger than that. You know it, finally, and you're bringing faith into your life, you're putting it into your mind and heart.

Yet, there is a hole! There's still something nagging at you and I'm going to reveal it, so you can avoid any traps or pitfalls. I'm talking about how to properly receive faith.

You see, many people just allow faith to happen. The plans are absent. The goals are missing. There's this intellectual understanding, and "lip service" but no real action. Your faith does not change or grow because you don't change or grow. Do not fret. This is natural.

I never promised instant faith. It's not a "just add water" situation. Surely, it can happen, and it's already been happening as you've made progress with everything you've already learned. But a true abundance of faith requires an abundance of action. Like for like. Again, it's similar to energy.

So, you know how to get started. That merely takes some action. Go back and revisit anything you don't fully understand. But, abundance is different.

Here's a quick story. My mind opened up a while back. I was thinking about how we really learn best. I realized the answer was obvious. I thought of all the times I taught something. I had a vision of being a teacher. I didn't see myself as a student, but as someone who needed to explain the process of faith, then it all was so obvious.

If you want to receive unlimited amounts of faith into your life, you must be ready, willing and able to receive that faith... through your ability to clearly teach it. You need to know it, you need to see it. Deeply. Faith in action must be very, very obvious to you. You must see the gifts in life, from life, and about life, all around you. You are an eternal, divine teacher.

What's more, you must be willing to receive faith through the actions of others. Think about how you feel when you receive gifts on your birthday or a holiday. How you receive that gift is profoundly important. Do you appreciate the gift? And, do you feel thoughtfulness? Do you literally say thank you? Are you embarrassed? Are you uneasy? Faith in action is very similar.

Now, you have the building blocks. Teaching is an action. That's faith in motion. Teaching is the best way of learning something. You know faith best when you teach it. You can think of teaching faith as faith itself. And, you can think of listening to others teaching faith as faith as well. Like many things in life, you are forever a teacher and student. Always giving, always receiving.

This also explains why faith is infinite. If you teach someone, you are a teacher. But, you are also a student of your own life, of that faith as action. It's a loop. Plus, when others teach you about their faith, you are a student, and you gain new knowledge that you can, in turn, teach to others. This is another loop.

Is it any wonder that two circles, side by side, form the infinity symbol? One circle is infinite. Two circles, joined, are still infinite. You might even see in your mind, and feel in your body, the true depth of infinite infinity.

Don't laugh.

There is finite infinity! For example, there are literally an infinite number of numbers between 0 and 1, such as 0.5, 0.25, 0.1, and so on. This alone might cause your mind to melt a bit. But, I bring this up because of a critical point I'm about to share.

If you are selfish, and do not share your learning, your gifts, and your life, you are acting in a universe of finite infinity. It's powerful, but it's a single closed loop. It's zero and infinity, at the same time. But, if you are not selfish, and you share what you've earned, and your gifts, and you share your life, you and life become infinite infinity.

The radical shift is that if you want to receive unlimited, infinite living faith, then you must be prepared to share. You must be willing to go outside yourself, into the world, into the full expanse of reality, and even beyond reality. Sharing is caring about your faith.

Again, the only caution is that you refrain from pushing your actions of faith on others. As you know, those students with closed eyes and ears are not ready. But, the time will come. Be patient with them. Be patient and gracious with yourself too, of course.

Remember, before you started this small journey with me, you were blind to many ideas. Some of these ideas are so big, and run so deep, that others will run away in fear. Others need more of a foundation. Still others simply need more time. Let them teach you, because remember, every single person has faith. They do! Remember, we all have faith, every one of us.

Faith Always And Everywhere

You are near the end of this part of your journey with me. But, before I go, please allow me to share some final thoughts.

If you still lack faith, or if you don't understand what I've explained in many ways, then I encourage you to focus on a single powerful word: yet.

According to Carol Dweck, the power "yet" gives students a path into their future and makes them feel that they are not stuck in some dead end. To always be growing, you can therefore literally just add the word "yet" to the end of your comment or feeling.

You turn… I don't have faith into…I don't have faith yet.

You convert… I don't understand faith into… I don't understand faith yet.

You change… I don't teach living in faith into… I don't teach living in faith yet.

This can be used in any situation where you have a genuine desire to increase any dimension of faith. Even better, you don't need some powerful belief to make it work. You merely need to understand that you are a work in progress.

You only need a simple, actionable mechanism. With the automatic energy of "yet" you only need to believe that you are alive. If you believe you are alive, and I bet you do, then you know that life changes. You know that life will go on. You know, without question, that you are taking action. So, you're riding the wave, instantly preparing for improvement.

I also ask that you follow the idea provided by Gustav Jacob Jacobi. He is known for the Jacobi inversion formula, where you flip things upside down, or reverse them. So, for example, if you lack faith, you write down all the reasons you have no faith whatsoever. Fantastic! Because by taking action on this, by moving, you're increasing your faith. You're learning more about how faith works, the barriers you see, and then you can even invert these objections. You can do this over and over, building faith, since faith is life in motion.

Of course, the cynic will point out that you might pound in negative thoughts and ideas, or that you find more faults in your faith. This is rational and reasonable. But, wouldn't you agree that it's impossible to fully answer a question without a complete understanding of the challenge? It's impossible to do addition if you don't even have the numbers to add together.

Bringing the unknown into the light brings awareness. Like faith, awareness isn't so much a thing as it is a process. The same could be said for any kind of enlightenment. And, a little bit of work goes a very long way.

As a final note, you were born in faith. Literally, you were physically born through faith. I'm talking about the mother, father, doctors, nurses, hospital and more. I'm also talking about those who came before, such as grandparents, and other family members.

Consider, even before you were born, complete strangers believed in you. They expected someone exactly like you to be alive, in motion. Maybe as a neighbor. Maybe as a co-worker. Maybe as a friend. We believe in humanity, before that humanity appears.

We also easily turn our faith into love. Sometimes, as you know, faith is represented as truth, plain and simple. Maybe, it manifests as a wish. Other times, faith shows itself as hope. But, it's rare that true faith, deep faith, will be negative or evil. Faith wins, because life wins, as we are always in motion.

I trust... I wish... I hope...

And, above all, here, right now,

At this very moment...

More than ever before...

I have faith that you HAVE FAITH.

Made in the USA
Columbia, SC
16 November 2023